SIGNED COPY

£2.99

F ②

ghost on the road

To Henrietta

poetry

Do enjoy!

Best

John C.

john clarke

28/9/2006

tall-lighthouse

To the lasting memory of cherished parents, Jack and Olive.

Heartfelt thanks to Martin Robinson, my editor at *tall-lighthouse*, for his unwavering engagement and industry.

Thanks are due to the editors of the following magazines for publishing my work: *Unpublished, The Polka Dot Ceiling, Greenwich Pirate*.

Some of these poems were previously published in *Travelling Without Arriving* (tall-lighthouse 2001) and *Jazz & Other Religions* (tall-lighthouse 2002/2005) and *tall-lighthouse poetry review* (2004)

Cover image and photo: Emma Bahar

ISBN 1 904551 23 8

published by
tall-lighthouse
www.tall-lighthouse.co.uk

contents

Jazz

Flipside

Spontaneous Combustion

Sensitive Areas

Every time I open my big mouth,
I put my soul into it.

Bob Kaufman

Jazz

Synchronicity

Shadows everywhere
of music once heard
that nothing can recapture
where boundaries are blurred

where did the notes go
memory playing aural tricks
James Moody, George Coleman
Lockjaw, Maceo Parker

bouncing bent shadows off a wall
somewhere in a downtown bar
not shadows of former selves
but a cluster of jewelled memories
dusted off, freed from static

dig out the original vinyl
see if it works the magic
put the genie back in the bottle
watch time as it disappears
into the music

Drummer Man

Necks shake loose from bodies
at Brixton's 'Jamm'
while I revel in the visual
sweet sonic syncopation
of a rotunda style Gene Krupa solo
replete with seductive echoes
of steamy jungle nights

as newsline: *Gene Krupa is arrested*
flashes up on screen
gaunt heroin cheeks dark circles
round the eyes, white but not quite
his cut-across quavers held the sharpness
of a needle plunging in his arm

cold information from a life so hot
it self-combusted with breezy wanton
magnificence, compounding insistent
switchback rhythms and riffs
twisted sermons from the mount
of Jazz and Swing
skips, chops and hammer pumps
from the palms of a manic lizard

percussive soar into the long dark night
impacted rumble roll and roar
with the smear of a smile
the king of the skins reigns supreme
his family a tympani of dazzling kith and kin

gimme just a few more crazy minutes
with good ol' crazy Gene
just a few more crazy minutes
with crazy crazy Gene
jaws circulating gum, savage glint in the eye
that's what I want, just a few more
crazy minutes with sweet crazy Gene

how his scar does linger
across the face of jazz
like a gypsy's curse

Dizzy Happenin'

If you're not out there
you're not doin' it
to be or not to bop, to be or not to bop
you been busy and dizzy... dizzy and busy
to be or not to bop, to be or not to bop
hang those horses n' let me off
this is my stop
to be or not to bop, to be or not to bop
sit tight n' let it happen
someone else pullin' those strings
all kind of won'erful things
got you firin' on all cylinders
flashbulbs shootin' off all over town
to be or not to bop, to be or not to bop
from Shakespeare to the Statue of Liberty
from the Louvre to Amsterdam
to be or not to bop
it ain't ever been enough
to be or not to bop
your time has come so
sit back n' let jazz take you
to all those places you ever wanted to go
let it wash over you at the drop of a hat
then don't ever look back
to be or not to bop, to be or not to bop
pile it on my plate it's inactivity I hate
to be or not to bop
blessed be the call
to man woman child n' all
to be or not to bop
your time has come
and it ain't ever gonna stop
no it just ain't ever gonna stop
this is jazz, not hip hop
never gonna stop, no never gonna stop
to be or not to bop, to be or not to bop
keeps you busy and dizzy, dizzy and busy
to be or not to bop, that IS the question

Defiant gesture

The devil of my own making comes to call
and I tell him to go away
the way my mother would:
Be off with yourself!
his laughter haunts me still.

Waiting for the silence to evaporate
like a wished for temptation
wrapped in seclusion
and a formulated spirit
of a winter that will not disappear.

A luscious Hodges alto solo
slides me into January
like a leaf beneath the front door,
the plaintive lilting register
commands attention but all too soon
is drowned by too lush an accompaniment
until finally it wriggles free
with a signature obbligato
fading away like tinsel
from a Christmas tree.

The less you think about jazz
the more you enjoy it.

A Jazz Supreme

So I'm up here on the bandstand listening
to the man telling me how I should blow
I say to him listen here man you're just
a good-for-nothing know everything
know nothing so-and-so
I heard Lockjaw play howling tenor
then switch to tender ballads from nine to three
midwinter out by the icy Baltic sea
in a dive in Aarhus one dark Tuesday.

All I regret is how I missed the duet
with him and Dizzy on the Saturday
after he'd recorded that same afternoon
over in Malmo for Steeplechase.
So don't talk to me about pace
and rhythm and majestic harmony
'cos I've seen it, breathed it, lived it,
sucked more of it into my system
than you'll ever know.

Time I know is one helluva stealer
but rhyme'n'rhythm married together
become an instant healer,
just try a dose of it and you'll
catch on quick to what I'm sayin',
it's got to be a whole lot better
than lowering yourself down
upon your knees a-mumblin' and a prayin'
at the altar of worthless dreams.

Do you realize man
that Woody Herman
and his Herd played
in this here toilet last week?
I just saw you cats jumpin' and I thought
I'd squeeze a bit more energy and zip
into the solo so I went for it.

The worst thing you can do man
is to play the music and not listen
to the crowd - you got to listen out
for the crowd - 'cos it's their reaction
that dictates and sets the pace,
controls the whole barometer
of excitement in the joint, so whenever
you play the golden rule is: *listen.*

When I left that club it was like
the ghostly silence after midnight mass
and as I looked behind all I could see
was a map of my firm footprints
in the freshly-fallen snow.
and all I could hear was a night
of thoughts, memories, words and sounds
that have rung through my ears ever since.

Late Trane Blues

Drummer Roy Haynes said that: 'playing with John Coltrane was like a beautiful nightmare'

I want to taste the blossom falling
from the dark petals of his lips
to live within the secret depths
of harmonic reminders that fade out reality
to pray at the melodic altar of his dreams
as they delve into the distant paranoia
of anguished oblivion

I want to withstand the moody melancholy
of his soulful explosions
to sweep the backyard of tenements
littered with the biting integrity
of his artistry
to sleep beside
the restless fathoms
of his speechless heart

I want to journey with him
into realms of the impossibly spiritual
to hitch my soul onto his wagon
of wailing arpeggios sprouting
a sorcerer's spell
to crouch behind
the expressive ligature
of surging glissandos

I want the world to stop and listen
to him and all those other high priests
and priestesses of jazz
to cry with him as if they too held
the collapsed wings of a homeless bird
then wake in a desert
with his devouring eyes
guiding the eternal drift and fusion
of their bodies

I want to hear the muffled gasp
as savage *sheets of sound* rip thru the roof
to unlock the cave door
of the devastated spirit
to smell the sweet obsession
as it moulders in the ground
then watch as the sky opens
to welcome him in
and share the lonely portal
of his beautiful nightmare

What jazz can do (for your life)

jazz is a master of disguise, jazz soars - jazz dives
to many jazz might seem a straight obscenity
to aficionados, it's the hip road to truth
and the cool path to serenity
jazz stems from the heart
it's a fluid agile muscular art
it's ripple and flow attached to heavy undertow
it's roar - it's rock - it's rage all at once
on a moving floating performance stage
it's candour - it's glamour - it's camouflage
weeping sweeping seeping timing to perfection
whatever your predilection
jazz gives jazz takes jazz lives but never fakes
and always offers maximum protection
it's cutting edge - a tilted window ledge
a book that holds a vast store
of musical knowledge
jazz inspires jazz desires jazz fires but never dies
jazz makes you go weak at the knees
it's a hammer blow - a cosmic light show
a dreamy warm inner glow
jazz teaches you what you want to know
it takes you where you want to go
shake hands with jazz for a lifelong friend
fall in love with jazz and you've got someone
who'll stay with you right thru to the bitter end
jazz is something you can't ignore
so make jazz the first knock upon your door
and know jazz is the security
you've been longing for
set against other religions
you may be inclined to follow
jazz makes many of them seem lacking in rhythm
short on life shallow and hollow
so choose jazz as your partner to jazz up your life
jazz soars - jazz dives
jazz is a master of disguise

Hip Heaven

There's a cooking quartet in a cellar bar
booze smoke a guy on his own motionless
taking in the scene
a cold-eyed discerning nobody
a girl a looker loosening up the joint
bare walls pockets of heavy silence
intimate alcoves an unidentifiable odour
music embracing every corner
trumpet vibrato hiss of cymbal
long languorous solos digging bass
spirited runs and breaks arriving at dead ends
staccato spurts of sound slicing
through rainbow ribbons of light

drummer and tenor
sucking on the neck of a bottle
cuff brushing lips
picking up the sense of
        nothing-in-particular going on

but knowing that wherever they are
the centre is here in Hip Heaven
where all roads are targeted
this common scenario
where no matter what the weather
is doing on the outside
those here on the inside are kicking up a storm
jumping those lights and laying down
        the law in musical notes
trailing tantalizing rhythms
a world away from all that hostile drama
happening elsewhere

Beat Blues

music is counting and not realizing that you're counting,
but when you realize that you're counting
then you're not making music

I never count the beats
I let the beats take care of themselves
the rhythm tells me where to stop
where to make a break
and when to rush right back in.

I can rustle up something
pretty darn quick
you don't see a time bomb
you only hear its tick
and what results can be tender
tough laid back or slick.

To make somethin' out of nothing
you wake up some lamb
on its way to the slaughter
and if you happen to be Italian
you're as lucky as sin
'cos you can make a decent meal
out of a solitary cup of water.

No I never count the beats
and can't stand all those heats
an athlete needs to seal victory
best set it down as you feel it
hear it picture it or see it
than leave a rusty line of promises
scattered down those dark roads of history.

So I never count the beats
somehow that smacks of self defeat
the beat is a resonance -
and you know when you've got it
the beat is jinglin' silent
change in your pocket.

The beat tells you when to start
and knows when to stop it
for me the beat should come
as natural as drawing breath
and by counting the beats
you simply hasten its death.

Said It Before I Read It

Skipping through *Mexico City Blues*
Kerouac praising Charley Parker, spells
it 'ley' not 'lie'. Glad I said it before I read it.
He even uses the same phrase: *Lidded eyes*
but I said it before I read it, hear that.

Gonna walk with his soul wrapped
around my body like a towel
gonna steam myself in the sauna
of his delivery, gonna guard against
cold winds whistling down my spine,
gonna go with his mind on a journey,
accept no lifts from strangers.
Anyone asks I live out over
on the other side, other side of that hill,
that valley, that river, that long dirty dusty road.

And if anyone else asks
I said it before I read it.
I'm true to my word,
ask Kerouac ask Bird
I said it before I read it.

I just wanna blow some jazz
in a jam on a Sunday afternoon
in a windowless room
using the pale aura
and instant karma of Kerouac
flying with the frantic melody of Bird.

Did you get it?
I said it yes I said it baby
I said it before I read it
and if you didn't listen
then there's no way you could
have heard.

The Nod

You think he's on the nod
        but he's not
he's listening and he's watching
he's cookin' away inside wonderin'
        which note to play next

when he's ready he'll
        give the signal
he won't say a word
        not the flicker of an eyebrow
not a wink of his left eye
        not the faint motion of a hand

he'll just show the pencil
        of a smile
then he'll nod
        just nod

The way I like my jazz

I don't want my jazz on Sunday with brunch
give me jazz with rhythm and a knockout punch

I don't want my jazz with steak and fries or grills
give me jazz that kicks me in the guts with its
hip tunes and thrills

I don't want my jazz in a hotel lounge
with dimsum Thai
give me jazz that flies tears the friggin' roof
off the sky

I don't want my jazz with pizza this or pizza that
give me jazz that blows me off my stool
and lifts my hat

I don't want jazz with sassy drinks
at nightclub prices
give me jazz that's down to earth
and let's me escape each day's fresh crisis

I don't want jazz that sits down
and demurely asks permission
give me jazz that stands up and takes off
like rocket-propelled nuclear fission

I don't want jazz that eats up
all my hard-earned dollars
give me jazz for free that bleeds the blues
then kicks n'screams n'hollers

I don't want jazz storing up
gold palaces of wealth
give me jazz for free on the National Health

I don't want jazz over on the other side of town
give me jazz right on my doorstep with those
dirty shades pulled down

I don't want jazz in a place
you gotta pay to be seen
give me jazz in a lowdown dive
the way it's always been

Give me jazz for free the way it ought to be
jazz for free for you and me
we're all of us messed up
and drownin' in the blues
so blow that sweet hurtin' sobbin' jazz
man you ain't got nothin' to lose

jazz for free for you and me
jazz for free the way it has to be
jazz the way it is now is a tax known as stealth
so lets have goddamned free jazz
for the masses on the National Health

Uncommon Artistry

Listening to Charlie Parker play
Lover Man in 1946 as he looked
for the drugs he couldn't get
trying desperately to forget.

A fragile tune by a fragile man
toting a twisted horn,
shivering from withdrawal,
eager to mask eternity's tears
drenching his sloping shoulders,
tombstone eyelids closed
in serene benediction.

He produced a haunting jazz classic
that ungraciously he came to frown upon
and never wanted released.

Perhaps it all-too-evidently,
as each note unfurled, revealed the pain
and damage like an unbandaged open wound.

Then, hidden depths of sadness,
fury that pounded the brain.

Bird had a special way
of attacking the melody, detonating a note
that was odourless, tempered, timeless.

As soon as you thought you had it pinned
it was gone, flown like the fleeting
days of childhood.

What lingered in the mind was the sound,
the monumental player and the sound,
the gut-balling inside that wrenched
the heart, seeped within the psyche,
tore the unruffled feathers from a flightless bird.

What you receive is the gnarled anguish
and intensity of pain
of an uncommon musical artist in performance,
emotionally drained, dying on his feet,
relaying his splintered life story through his reed
whilst somehow maintaining that effortless
redemptive god-given improvisational style.

Musical milestones do not lie
but, like this take or Brubeck and Desmond's
Take Five or Monk's *Round Midnight*
remain supremely faithful,
indelibly loyal to that unrepeatable moment.
The musician's true meaning may be blamed
but never shamed.

Lush Life for a Pittance

I begin the day regretting
that I missed band leader
and alto sax giant Lou Donaldson
play at the Jazz Café
on Monday and Tuesday.

After dropping off a few odds and ends
at the local charity shop
I perform my usual quick shuffle and shufti
through the tired pile of cassettes
filling the box on the counter;
within seconds I'm clutching
a home-made tape marked at a princely 50p
featuring a pair of Blue Note recordings
from a decade back.

On one side is a live Kenny Dorham
Round About Midnight at the Café Bohemia
which turns out to be ace
while the other side contains the very man
Lou Donaldson's *Lush Life* album
featuring classic renditions of *Stardust,*
The Good Life, It Might As Well Be Spring
and other gems I've yet to identify
as there is no full listing.

What's that about coincidence being God's
unsuccessful attempts to remain anonymous?

I believe I do really and truly believe
as I wallow in the lush life acquired for just 50p,
ninety minutes worth of breezy, bluesy nostalgia
for far less than the price of a three minute
corporate coffee that tastes like mush.

Switching the tape over again
a trumpet enters with an amazing blues hook
that shreds the heart
like some half-forgotten memory
lying inside a Pandora's box of dreams.

Suddenly the music stops
as Kenny Dorham approaches the microphone
Thank you very much ladies and gentlemen, now
at this time we'd like to play Autumn in New York.

Days of innocence in the midst
of poverty, insecurity and violence
long before you know what
long before.

Chameleon

All through the jazz symphony
A Love Supreme, Coltrane weaves
in and out of intricate shadows
like a chameleon gasping for breath,
locked in a dream, aghast in a wilderness.

Every move, each tortured beat
is a journey through light
plunging into darkness,
desolate, arid, significant
then back toward the light.

Spun rhythms flung like discarded garments
into the farthest reaches of desperate infinity
cry broken tears of dread isolation.

A coded integrity of form through licks of sound
asserts essential phrases of rhythm and chant
that revolve in brilliant puddles of uncertainty.

Perfect alignment of spirit
with modulation of tone
defining expanding destiny.

Suddenly the blind leaves dissolve
to reveal shades of soundless silence
within *A Love Supreme* that everyone
can warm to, where no one need feel afraid
the mystery of music, ceaseless as the motion
of the sea, drums, bass, piano, horn.

Flipside

Revelation Blues

It's the sudden realisation
that you've done it all, seen it all
couldn't go back if you tried.

It's a twisted situation
a little short on liberation
a fox stops dead in its tracks
impudently looking back at you.

It's a wonder you've lasted this long,
most the time the song is the same
crazy laughing rambling song -
you go away but soon you're longing
to get back where you belong.

It's the therapy you've chosen
or maybe the treatment chooses you -
the bus arrives shining its headlights
in your eyes like time catching up on you.

It's the lazy inclination
that you've been there, seen it all before
and all your cats change colour in your memory,
every day is just another jet trail
bothering a blue sky.

It's that haunted house
they warned you about
sat up on windy hill
it's the pocketful of nothings you've left
once you've realised that words can kill.

The Meaning of Hip

To be hip is to constantly face the blank canvas
read chants from a silent hymnbook
air strings of grievances in a fogbound airport
fold up the text and leave all belongings behind
forget the existence of barricades and barcodes
dream of the ancient rites of solitude
level with a square world

discard the ashes of the past
          into the trashcan of tomorrow
embrace all you ever wanted beyond
          the vague limits of vile disappointment
cherish worthwhile achievements
as if they were an epiphany of diamonds
          inhabiting a nightmare of happy accidents

carry the orgasm of the word in the sacred
ciborium of the intellect
until the urge to release proves uncontrollable

feel the penetrating sigh
of each human association
for even a nanosecond harmony or discord
skate across the floor of a million emotions
                    then say nothing
scream at the whipped dog of failure
as though it were a botched abortion
grind to dust those eternal verities
          once held inviolable

hip is being in permanent mental distress
due to excessive displays
of obsessive moral foreplay
avoiding the false redemption of arty bollocks

hip is flip a coin for the colour flavour texture
of a ready-made irreversible goddamned
beautiful cosmic destiny

hip knows it can't possibly win but keeps on
trying all the same

hip will recant when hell itself freezes over

Bob Dylan

Let me sit here forever
and listen to your song
you say you know it well
so it won't take long
lies are the biggest truth
your body a blur
drowned out by a gospel choir.

The flood of possibilities
thuds into a wall of silence
co-ordinates of nobodies
reflected on a page of twisted lyrics.

A red silk dress
laid across a kitchen table
a strange token of immutability
and time passing slowly
a fevered response
to a new morning.

Another dreamscape ready to unravel
ravages of complicity and betrayal
another girl from the north country
wearing an Egyptian ring
with a red stone, a wealth of stories
and no direction home.

I'll be in your dream if you'll be in mine
the artist is excused for running out of steam
I'll be waiting on desolation row
for tambourine man
to coincide with your cosmic vision
of the apocalypse.

Point of View Corkscrew

Roger from Liverpool says his son's
a handsome brute, a quarter Cherokee
and fully six foot seven - guess that's
some babe's idea of heaven
but that makes his mother half Cherokee
- hey now you're talkin'!

what is life? I don't know -
life's all you dare dream of
then the lights go out
it's the crack up before the crackdown
then the circus comes to town

it's the way this poxy 172
never gets ahead of that poxy 21
it's the girl next to the girl next to the girl
in the next room
it's a spent match the dream you catch
an upturned waste bin
an ice-bucket that's lost its sparkle

a freshly amputated limb
a flamboyant wrecking-crew
a ball that never stops rolling

that song you could have written
a hearse with the disco lights full on
and the DJ spinning *All Right Now*
hands still soaked in the juice
of last night's kebab
with his girlfriend bemoaning
how he can never find her clitoris in the dark
as he pokes a serene right hook
thru the broken window of her screams

New Cross

The Devil's Island of South East London
always hustling trying to survive
on out-of-date travel card
a packet of impoverished Rizlas
and tinny personal stereo
ah but the devil as always
looks after his own.

When the Old Kent Road gives up the ghost
there lies the ravages and rust of New Cross
destinations are inevitable
but how do you find them when no maps
of the area exist
where blood's extruded from lifeless bodies
and chalk is the colour of my true love's stare.

Drowsy *Café Crema* looks positively threatening
with its gunmetal shutter rammed down
in daylight, so violent is the daubed graffiti
overlooking the main road
with its horny flow of traffic
the library opens on alternate days
Iceland never seems to shut.

Side roads contain nothing
but shades of empty sadness
bordering on the loveless
festooned with cheap digs
and anonymous parked vehicles.

Funkily-dressed students and sombre musos
ferry guitar cases for soundchecks
headed for *Music City*
an early sesh at *The New Cross Inn*
Amersham Arms, The Montague
Goldsmiths Tavern or the college bar
or gigs in the wide world beyond SE14.

Others pour off the free bus
- two to choose from in New Cross
a trumpeter acquaintance calls them
the performing artist's chauffeur
ever-popular and 24 hour
in a city that boasts about supporting
grass roots culture then mostly shits
on the vast body of those who
speed the pulse beyond caring
only to be enervated on a daily basis.

Halloween approaches so camp witches
and ghouls along with a heavily made up
Frank 'n' Furter figure clad in fishnets
and sussies adorn the windows of *Rubbish Fairy*
where the owner told me she was expecting
which makes a welcome change
for the one thing you really miss in New Cross
is that redeeming air of expectation
she once gave me a fiver for a pair of pale
blue 70's adidas waterproof trainer-bottoms.

New Cross anaemic analeptic life enhancing
where even beneath that scaly scutter
of *The Venue* there's another venue
sprouting thru the floorboards.
London's like that, below the surface
always something worthwhile occurring
Haven't you heard? someone
has scrawled by a block of peeling posters
New Cross is the new Seattle don't cha know?

Don't use after the sell-by date

Let me bleed into the low-slung holster
          of your saltfish memory
dream alongside the wildly-reduced value
          of that scantily-clad
                    joint bluechip portfolio
while cupping the upturned saucers
          of your breasts
until I go suddenly boss-eyed with longing.

Let me blow into the velvet cheeks
          of your primed and loaded
                    crowded aspirations
to kiss away all those crude debit entries
          on your credit card statement
tell the birds to swallow them whole
          then regurgitate them
on politicians' breakfast plates.

Let me harness the grated sawdust that cakes
          your eyelids and throw open the covers
of your silence refreshed by showers of rain
     so you dance forevermore to every moon
that shows upon each crumpled
                         bleached horizon.

Take me where scattered hearts lie sheltered
          by the wind
join me on that lampless journey
          down jazz-haunted streets
to the dying echo of a Cootie Williams cry
          that pitches us both onto the
ever-spinning cartwheel of another planet
where things happen when you want them to.

Beneath the umbrella of the aurora borealis
where we sink into the intermittent
warmth and sadness of a deep southern blues
blistered by the sun
laced with low-grade whiskey
that shoots straight from the hip
to the gut filling every empty cavity
in between.

Honey you know for sure
that it's the god's-own-truth
with a little pinch of pig-meal on the side
just a tiny pinch of pig-meal on the side.

Then let me wake beside you to find
the turquoise-gold of lanterns
drifting across the scorching phantoms
of your eyes
drawing out the pain of the plantations
and agree that all the spent
shells in history
were simply one long line of people
masturbating bullets
compared to the hot sweet trail
of sealing-wax
dribbling down the inside
of your rippling thighs.

Bird of Passage

Bird dust caking the backs of my legs
exposing the drama of everything and nothing
the hourly pretensions and inventions
we remorselessly convey
with the ease of angels
Buddha music
everything and nothing.

I am a nihilist and a realist
I don't have a cock as thick as your wrist
don't drive a Shogun people carrier
can't escape the virus that infects the brain
know days in advance when it's going to rain.

Coal dust belching through gaping holes
            in memory
hitting the pit of the stomach
emptying the sack
creating a dark pool of slack
smeared on the cheeks like war paint
practising for a moustache
stomping of horses' hooves
on swollen tarmac.

Jay-thrush tan back picturesque mauve neck
blue black and white tipped feathers
perched momentarily before disappearing
in flight into a clump of trees -
a bird of passage leaving its indelible mark
everything and nothing.

The Glove Compartment

I know a churning crowded
messy vaguely pointless
sort of black hole called
the glove compartment of life
where I'm always looking
for that creased and crumpled
map of my favourite provincial town
and those pair of dusty grimy
Ambre-Solaire smeared Polaroids
I haven't seen for years - strange
I never seem to turn up any gloves.

The Present

It is the past.
Paris has just been liberated.
Europe's constricted horizons still groaning.
Hemingway calls on Picasso
at his house-cum-studio
in the rue-des-Grands-Augustins.

The faithful concierge reports that
Picasso is away. In his absence
the writer wants to leave a message
for the artist.

The housekeeper suggests that
un petit cadeaux would be
more appropriate.

The man of action acts swiftly
and from the back of his jeep
removes a box of live grenades
scrawling the message
to Picasso from Hemingway.

The old lady immediately takes flight
once she realises the form of the present
the taciturn stranger has left
in the dingy hallway.

Presumably Picasso saw the funny side
having already depicted in scalding detail
the blind horror of war in his Guernica canvas.

Spontaneous Combustion

Visions of Kerouac

I see Kerouac as the dead heart
of a shielded future,
an open page with scornful frown
enlightened by stillness,
bolstered by the stiffening breeze
a still beating insurgent heart
that glows in the dark like a rose
an apple or the sacred host.

The beat heart of a deadbeat
who sings the blues
down the jaded throat of jazz
blowing coded chords
thru the long captive night of the soul
like some schizoid avenging angel
lashed to the mast of a ship
adrift on an ageless ocean.

Face shaved hair freshly parted
face so packed with meaningful expression
it makes you tremble
face of America trying to make sense
of everything that has happened.

Messages from drunken blowflies

I fly thru sandstorms of rainbows
beating with red hot pokers of words
hurled from the turrets of burnt out castles
onto the cracked lips of passing camel trains.

I find my brains in a bag of lost belongings
parading round a carousel of foreign holidays
sun-kissed as ancient ruins
floating on islands of heartbeats
or wet as the unpressed creases of eggshells
on a broken morning
where language sleepwalks
thru overhead skies
choked with the dust-laden wings of Angels.

I disappear into childhood gardens
where mist traps the bleached undergrowth
like a ferret in a one-way rabbit hole
looking for fragments of a misshapen
nursery rhyme
I haunt the dried up riverbeds of my
trackless memory where drunken blowflies
tap out reckless messages
toward the gnarled claws of
star-ravaged mountains.

Everybody's talking bout the Plastic Ono Band
making a comeback on the third moon of Orion
or in the bed of Gandhi on the 35th floor
of the Calcutta Hyatt Hilton
as servants ferried in fleets of stretch limos
go in search of goats milk and organic ghee
in the foothills of Bangalore
while the frozen frosts of rainbows
play a succession of unbroken
horn and drum solos.

I hammer into a wall composed
of the puffed up eyes of alligators
wipe my brow with a Hermes silk scarf
carved from the stripped down
innertubes of dead bicycles
where babies fall headfirst
into the isolated drop-zones
of basketball-playing paratroops.
as the shrapnel of broken hearts
explodes and echoes through
a speeding fandango of ageing foxholes.

I take off thru sandstorms of rainbows
beating with red hot pokers of words
dripping worthless syllables
hurled from the turrets of burnt out castles
onto the cracked lips of passing camel trains.

Cowboy boots

Swooping like magpies around the base camps
of sleeping pagodas cowboy boots
are makin' a comeback, worn by ladies I mean
pink turquoise tan and aquamarine
very Nancy Sinatra, very Barbarella
sexy as sin.

These boots are made for stalkin'
in soft flexible leather
perfect for truckin'
in this Indian Summer weather,
makes you want to walk about
in the sweet late summer sunshine
with all those rays drippin'
down on your back hell for leather.

Look there over yonder
it's sweet baby Jane Fonda
struttin' her stuff, lookin' all free
and kinda tough but underneath it all
she's gentle as a feather.

Dylan sent his lady all the way across the ocean
for those fine boots of Spanish leather -
may they always stay together
girls' legs and cowboy boots
in soft dreamy expanding leather.

There they go, diving like hawks
around the campfires of mountain gypsies
whose young women all look like
Linda Ronstadt in her prime
clad in that pair of white cowboy boots
with stitches and tassels way on down the line
you could feel the rising sap
she was the perfect man radar trap
perfect for truckin'.

These boots are made for stalkin'
these boots, these boots
are made for stalkin'.

Chinese lady, long flowing dark hair
taking the midnight air
outside Costcutters
and what does she wear?
a pair of Texan cowboy boots,
gives a whole new meaning
to puss 'n' boots

and there goes another pair
black with white squiggles
and all you can do is stare.

My Baby

my baby is a tar baby, my baby wants to know
what jazzmen are and I tell her
they're the battered sons of angels

my baby asks why do blues singers cry
and I say it's because they feel the pain
of history

my baby questions why some people
have more than others
and I reply that it depends
on what you're measuring

my baby says she likes to dance
to express her innermost feelings

I agree that's better than turning all bitter
angry n' twisted at the slightest problem

my baby thinks this place
is a dirty two-bit one horse town
I say to some it's sunny even when
it's a-rainin' down

my baby knows we're all on the same road
but not everyone is hip

my baby says I'm beginning to look
kinda louche

my baby loves the sound of pianos and seagulls
and how they reflect life's natural biorhythms
and makes her think of islands isolation
and vast empty skies

my baby is eager to learn whatever it takes
and wants to do what's right for all our sakes

first she'll examine the deep battle scars
of those lives drenched in Hot Jazz & Raw Blues

then she'll take a long hard breath
throw off her clothes, go walkin' in the rain
without any shoes

(I warn her to watch out
for cry baby Johnnie Ray)

maybe I'll join her one day
if I can ever shake off
these goddamn weary blues

yeah maybe I'll just go join my baby
if I can ever beat off these empty shotgun blues
where did I put my smokes
hand me that bottle of booze
I just wanna get loaded blues

my baby help me
cos I still got those
restless senseless
weary empty
shotgun blues

Cities that never sleep

Dinosaurs seep thru the water pipes
undermining the efforts of those
perpetually engaged in the unarmed combat
of futile imaginings
your girlfriend wants to know what's happening
as you swim in the ill-fitting
dress of her unlocked desires.

At night, buses sleepwalk thru mile upon mile
of deserted villages,
down boulevards of splintered glass
drowning in flyblown mysteries
chased by liberal armies of burst balloons
wielding broken walking sticks
stolen from run-down nursing homes.

There's a bulging mattress of discarded
shadows crowding the stinking stairwells
of dog-meat factories where Harry Potters
fear to tread as the underground underclass
curl up with rodents and sharpen their teeth
on the eyes of strangers
filing away intrepid national insurance numbers
in fireproof cabinets of a Legoland
of obsolete virus-ridden computers.

Steam disappears into the smoke of silence
as tributes of lame expletives explode
against the unwary double-glazed dreams
of catnappers who catch blazing-doll molotovs
hurled from high-rises, standing like
unquenched question marks in the smouldering
ruins of a 60's planner's nightmare
as copious lists of excuses are drawn up
by clenched fists declaiming a national disgrace
only to be flatly ignored by the guilty parties
since scattered to Biarritz Miami Hawaii
or similar five star hotels of the apocalypse.

As the eternally perplexed wonder why
they can never escape from the mistakes
of others and why the vast majority of lives
are so easily depleted and deflated
and why supreme control never ensnares
the muddy and muddled rabidly uncontrolled
who freely roam dwell and swell in our midst
like a cancer that's yet to be discovered.

No return

It's foolish I know
but emerging from the darkness
there's a sense of no return
sparkling ruins, featureless expressions
a landmark question hangs in the air.

Speak to a friend's 87 year old mother
still sound as nine pence, later, see photo
of her hefting a shiny Black & Decker drill
mending a broken fence, again
the burning sense of no return.

What magnetises that web of stolen moments
moving from solitary to gregarious
in the blink of an eye?
a stub of personality held permanently
on standby masking the feeble
sense of no return.

Mountains of books to be shifted cleared
and sifted, going back nigh on 40 years
of accumulated text images and ideas,
a massive cull is imperative
unpeel space, draw back time
yet the lingering sense of no return
with unread books ready to be discarded.

The vanity of hopes and wishes is only
part of what you learn
perhaps that's why it's always there
that tangible sense of no return
the way someone in your life disappears
never to be seen again
the reason you fail to recognize love
or regard it conversely as your mortal enemy.

Lorca, Berryman and Pasolini
envisioned dramatic death
and how it goes hand in hand
with an apocalyptic sense of no return,
that strange imperious sense of no return.

Multiplechoice Poem

sell your soul to the outcast
mixing up the dough
swap your brains with the devil
scuttering in the snow
sell your fugacious beauty
to Rooti van Houti
sell your fragile body
to a veritable also-ran
swap your island face
for the Turin shroud
and drink red wine as you sit
sprawled in the rain

write poetry when you feel like it
and eat at the café on the corner
when you got money in your pocket
smile all day and drift along easy
with that friendly early breeze
and don't let 'em tell you it's turkey
when you know it's only stale cheese

live every second on the line on the brink
but don't ever try to tell
a rocking-horse how to think
gather up all those stolen
empty shells of existence
lay 'em down before your feet
and give supreme thanks
for the resonant power
and fluidity of your agile conscience

there's a certain move afoot
to resurrect Forster's theory
of *only connect*
but how will it survive the exacting
leprosy of the collective intellect?

Fetish

there's no unhappier creature on Earth than a fetishist
who yearns for a woman's shoe and has to embrace
the whole woman — *Karl Kraus*

there's something about four-inch heels
worn with a pair of straight designer denims
that does things to me

when a shapely girl parks herself
on a nearby seat
and balances delicately as a stork

I go comatose
at the sight of those
sharply elegant elongated stilettos

this particular girl is perched
across the aisle
on the night bus

wielding the ultimate line
in branded accessory
like a lethal weapon

and for a brief spell, once the hordes
have decamped at the Elephant
as they usually do

she calmly stretches out both legs
wiggles her toes, then flashes
her chaotic chocolate brown eyes

knowing I am way
beyond
the point of redemption

the shoes are of the palest aubergine
diamante-edged with winkle-picker ends
you could slit a throat with

and in one tantalizing motion she swings
those slender pins fully 90 degrees
in my direction

and I swear the tips
momentarily brush
the fabric of my trousers

as I strain
to keep my gaze fixed
on the sign which reads

please give up these seats
to the elderly, the disabled
or those who have difficulty standing

now it might have been
pure wishful thinking
on my part

but when a young
slip-of-a-thing
boldly takes the initiative like that

you tend not to forget
the exalted experience -
night bus or no night bus

however I suspect
her two girlfriends
noticed something on the sly

and when they all began to discuss in detail
a recent brawl during some local
amateur football match

when a couple of the lads got stabbed
I suddenly lost all interest
in that ravishing pair of pointy shoes

and the girl with the Toblerone eyes.

Lemmy here

Lemmy was a character in the 50's cult radio show
'Journey Into Space'

travel in outer space
remains the last frontier
to feel the vital ultrasonic beep
and magnetic sweep of ultraviolet

ever the space cadet
I want to go to the blind adulation
of an all-girl Japanese rock band
throstling and screeching at full throttle
legs akimbo arms flailing
crotches thrusting like robotic tigers
drenched in spunk masquerading as dry ice
sprayed with the needless brainless
lyrics of deadly pop culture
that spawns tomorrow's apogees of terror
and experimental musical madness
with a furore as yet unglimpsed

still coming to terms with
the undignified haste of the space race
give me the pill that contains everything

I bought the fireworks
now I need to taste the real thing

if the space race still means anything
at all gimme the full blast off sensation
and lemme
go
with a w..h..o..o..s..h!

Horsepoem

Rimbaud you brilliant maniac stop dancing with camels
Bob Kaufman

The horses have stolen my liquorice
they know I live in a tree house
in a spooky forest
and am easily frightened
the doctor calls it a sickness
from which I may never recover

my body is engineered by monkeys
I am dumbfounded by the bleating
of mosquitoes; if I ever contract malaria
I will give it to the horses
          and blame the warble fly
because horses shit tow ropes from memory
win and lose races (check it out with Bukowski)
stand erect immobile then casually
          drop their faeces

make of your passions what you will
the sport of Kings'll make you
throw rocks at walls until they bounce back
never say hello in the dark
you won't hear the story if you don't sit still
the tattered heart doesn't own a sleeve
make your exit before you take your leave

and this poem is a horse that's lost
          its favourite saddle
the ultimate is to feel nothing
          touch no one
I remember the picture of the guttersnipe
          who hurled rocks at Black Beauty
see you on the shore, smack dab in the middle
preserve the link with angels on horseback

the horse flies on the wind
all strength confined to its hindquarters
fluid as poetry
          I smell liquorice

Obiter dictum

I have energies I never thought I had
I have weaknesses I should never admit to
I inhabit a road-movie winding its way
endlessly on shark-laden seas
in search of Le Palm d'or
I shoulder all the responsibilities
of a string of Dead Presidents.

I do not distinguish between murders
and assassinations, flee into dark corners
where even the rats won't go
take the temperature of narcissists
to prove they've outlived three hundred
different strategies for abject failure,
list the evidence produced
by eighteen pregnant stenographers
in four separate time zones
that famines are sinister examples
of population control.

I have memories to outstrip eternity
days I will never resurrect
I am not Lazarus nor Lapis Lazuli
I have skin ultra-sensitive to touch
I take out lawsuits just to see fragrant women
in flowing capes and white wigs
                with purple ribbons
recognise the healing power of chicken soup
I visit a remotely located bordello drenched
in darkness somewhere in pre-war
eastern Europe
I hear sung psalms as I stand erect in the
cathedral of burnt offerings
as I press my soul into the palm of the receiver
of cherished dreams attached to the magnet
of good fortune
and I listen out eternally for the grazed voices
of raised ambition as they ride out on reindeer
across late autumn skies.

Angela Jones speaks 17 languages

for Scott Gardiner

Angela Jones still a schoolgirl
somewhere in Wales
speaks 17 languages
tries out German French and Polish
on an opponent and meets her Waterloo
a gift of tongues not exclusively hers

hangs around bus-shelters with a pair
of spaced out hitch-hikers
straight out of *Withnail & I*

is this the ghost of Adrian approaching
tonight at noon fumbling with a garter
as he paints an idea that bleeds jazz into poetry
as Angela's voice keeps on shinin' thru?

Angela Jones brain like a well-oiled museum
quite a catch
it's a cool tongue that greets the morning dew
maddest half of the duo
strikes a match
hurls it on tinder doused in lighter-fuel
suddenly a blindin' flash and there
is no busshelter
not even a disused one with fluttering bunting
of edible panties

no more stompin' at the Savoy
on this bus-shelter
no more jumpin' at the Woodside
no more Saturday Night fish-fry
no more five guys named Mo
stirrin' up the grits steppin' out with Mr Bloe
this busshelter is endsville
kiss him goodbye
and 17 tongues have been hung out to dry

Sensitive Areas

You Ask Me

you ask me what takes the soul away
I tell you it is dreams

you ask me what takes the soul from here
I tell you it is falseness

you ask me what brings the soul on a journey
I tell you it is silence

you ask me what listens in the hallway
I tell you it is spirit

you ask me what rustles through the treetops
I tell you it is a sacred bird

you ask me what scurries through the fields
I tell you it is the meaning of lost souls

you ask me how I know such things
I tell you it is the blessedness of knowing

all in a manner of saying

Fatal Kiss

Some might blame Rodin or Cartier-Bresson, this was a fifteen year old girl from Quebec with a *nut allergy* who kissed her boyfriend full on the lips instead of giving him a peck not knowing that nine hours before he had some toast spread with peanut butter. Who would have imagined that a single kiss could bring down the shutter on a life barely begun despite a last-ditch shot of adrenalin?

Tichnoch, Cabinteely, Poulaphuca

Three villages in the Dublin Mountains whose names
my father would quote repeatedly like a mantra

It was always Cafolas on O'Connell Street
for the ice cream and the jukebox with those
wall-mounted selectors, Formica furniture
bordered with gleaming silver.

We'd spend what seemed like hours
inside that dazzling cathedral of a place
where none of the customers
put on painful airs or graces.

A dark-suited tousle-haired Glaswegian
stooped saying; *so ye like the Everly Brothers*
then laddie? in rhetorical fashion
after the duo's syrupy harmonies
poured out into a dreary Dublin afternoon.

Johnny he's a joker, he's a bird...
such a funny joker.... he's a bird dog
it's where you go where nothing ever happens:
Tichnoch, Cabinteely, Poulaphuca.

Sometimes I view my life as a storm
trying desperately to blow itself out
Tichnoch, Cabinteely, Poulaphuca
Tichnoch, Cabinteely, Poulaphuca.

Ding-dong

After a peaceful night's sleep
you awake to a rare old ding-dong
going on right above your head,
a door sounds as if it's being banged
off its hinges.

The anger and frustration of both parties
seems about equal as volleys
of choice repetitive expletives
cut the tepid Monday morning air
with animal ferocity.

At one stage she begins to phone
for the police then she's out on the balcony
hurling dog's abuse, wailing like a banshee
while he's down below 'giving it large'
as we used to say.

He wants all his 'stuff' left outside the door
she snorts that she knows all about him
and will tell the world; it's the usual
high-pitched high-frequency see-saw.

Neither will give ground
or take their foot off the pedal
they're both wound up like Mike Tyson
tearing into a helpless opponent.

Then without warning, like a typhoon's tail
the argy-bargy dies away to the earlier
halcyon calm, the solitary piece
of lame evidence is a sorry pair
of grubby dark tracksuit-bottoms
splayed across a brick wall at street level.

An hour or so later the street-sweeper
pushes his stiff bristly broom
rapidly along the pathway
and no-one is any the wiser.

Good-time gal

It's half one in the morning, drizzling rain at the bus stop waiting for the N89 to take me most of the way home. In the distance I see her striding jauntily down a semi-deserted Camberwell Church Street, bending to make a fuss of some old guy's labrador dog perfectly in tune with the proximity of the moment. As she draws level across the road she stops and flips her little denim jacket off her bare shoulders revealing a silver spangly top matched to a time-honoured come-hither smile. I give her the thumbs up and she responds by taking a couple of steps forward before posing in full suggestive profile; a few more moments then she jumps back into that skin-tight jacket and scoots purposefully away into the night. I'll never know whether she was worth missing that bus for.

Reading Stern

If you asked me what I lived for
I'd say it was for knowledge   *Gerald Stern*

I am transposing scratched-down notes from the backs of shopping receipts into a school-sized exercise book with funky geometric 70's shiny cover in cream and chocolate brown.

Reading Gerald Stern in a Turkish café on a windy morning a wind with bite a chittlin' wind. This is Stern's ninth collection and the first I've read. Stern is wonderful dry dramatic distinctive irrationally positive staunch supporter of nature he caresses words like a lover stacks them up irons them out all neat and tidy then shuffles the structure randomly until the pieces fit the way silence or commotion blends with certain seasons.

Stern is the latest hero extending borders touching wide extremities enlivening the process it is an opening a watershed an unsubjected entry into bliss an identifiable portion of paradise making poetry say what it's meant to say a munificent overtone like finding money on the ground scraps of starfish irresistible aperitifs for the longer works. It's all of a piece however you say it or present it an empty delirium a fogged picture of the past a fast track to knowledge wave upon wave of knowledge starshifts the irksome noise of memory ticking away.

With or without cocaine

I saw the terror forming in those mad eyes
it was Mau-Mau fear controlled by ECT
a back room with no escape
she was the victim I was the rape
used only a third of the required novocaine
her left foot balanced against the door frame
for extra leverage and swore
both hands gripping a plucky pair of pliers
minutes seemed like hours
led to one single vow: never to venture
into that dentists ever again.

It was as if she was trying to return
the evident pain and exasperation
of Africa directly to me,
with or without cocaine.

You might say she only wanted
to shake up my make-up but I know
she was only out to whup some ass,
might not be here had she been
let loose with the gas.

Her Voice *(people will say we're in love...)*

In the soft shaded undulating echoes of her voice
I recognise all the twists and turns,
ebbs and flows of the Potomac River
and hear the drowsing meadows
of its ruthless silence,
feel the hidden depths of long stretches
of unqualified conversations
over telephone wires connecting her to me.

There is a meaning, a scarcity
in that voice I can't explain
that tears at the very fibre of my being,
I am restless each time I hear it,
to have its warmth and engaging passion
forever beside me so that I can call on it,
be embraced by it whenever I want.

I now know the intimate ongoing
power of seduction,
she is the river that flows thru my heart,
its deft undeniable tributaries form my veins
and I am truly helpless
in the presence of such beauty
that sudden noble enticement that catches you
so unawares as the press-gang
of words towers above.

Her words are worth more than a stolen fortune
just as a dream one day marches forward
to become reality and you are pushed
somehow beyond finality.

Emptiness Blues

you can't go round saying bad things about
people, it's an unwritten rule
you fill one notebook then you fill
another
the day stumbles along somehow

thru bursts of writing scraps of food and
drink
memories of women future thoughts
of women
and you listen to some dated old-style
jazz
before trudging home on foot
a couple of miles

drumming it for all you're worth
which isn't much & serves to explain
why you're even drumming it
in the first place

then your right leg aches like billyo
and you need a warm hand to hold
guide you to bed and rest
your dick in its palm

times you wonder if you're living
at all
and whether you would be
better off dead

then the light wakes you
and you begin
the same old routine
all over again

it's coming on to summer
but it might as well be winter
and your mind is wandering all
over the place
and you haven't got a good thing
to say about anybody

Meditation upon Loss

when the spoken becomes unspoken
it is time to go in search of shadows

you feel the pressure to say the first
thing that enters your head

the way a line of English poetry
is shorter than most American

to rise up take a deep breath
hold it then mimic the dead

so much time spent reminiscing
upon a history where you do not belong

shelters exist for your use
but no one directs you to them

and nothing of significance will free
the frenzy of the forgotten moment

every poem becomes a dynasty
of sharpened syllables scored images

from the banal the memorable the flightless
the toneless to the plus *quam perfectum*

this may mean nothing unless you are
the priest who heard my last confession

Reading Bukowski

twenty poems to go
but I still want to turn
back to the beginning
in case I've missed
something bitterly
crucial,
before the rain spreads in
throughout
the country
and the music on the radio
turns sour